GET WELL SOON

No matter how dark the night
The sun will rise tomorrow.
I let hope be my guiding light
Through any pain and sorrow.

I wasn't wearing proper clothes
And now I've got a runny nose.
But with care I'll soon get better
And I'll wear a warmer sweater.

Healing can take some time
Until I'm feeling just fine.
I must be patient and wait a bit,
I can rest while I'm at it.

When "I" is replaced by "we",
"Illness" turns to "wellness", I see.
When I'm sick you show concern;
When I'm better, I'll take a turn.

When storm clouds cover the sky
The sun is still up high.
I rest assured that hope is there,
I ask God for help through prayer.

Difficult paths often end
with a beautiful view.
Feeling sick?
God will see you through.

DIFFICULT PATH

EASIER WAY

AMAZING VIEW

No matter how long the fall and winter,
Beauty follows with spring and summer.
God allows a time for each season;
I must trust that there is a good reason.

While riding fast and free,
I got injured on my knee.
What not-to-do I have learned
And some wisdom I have earned.

No more soccer for me,
At least not for a while.
But now I've learned to paint,
And that brings me a smile.

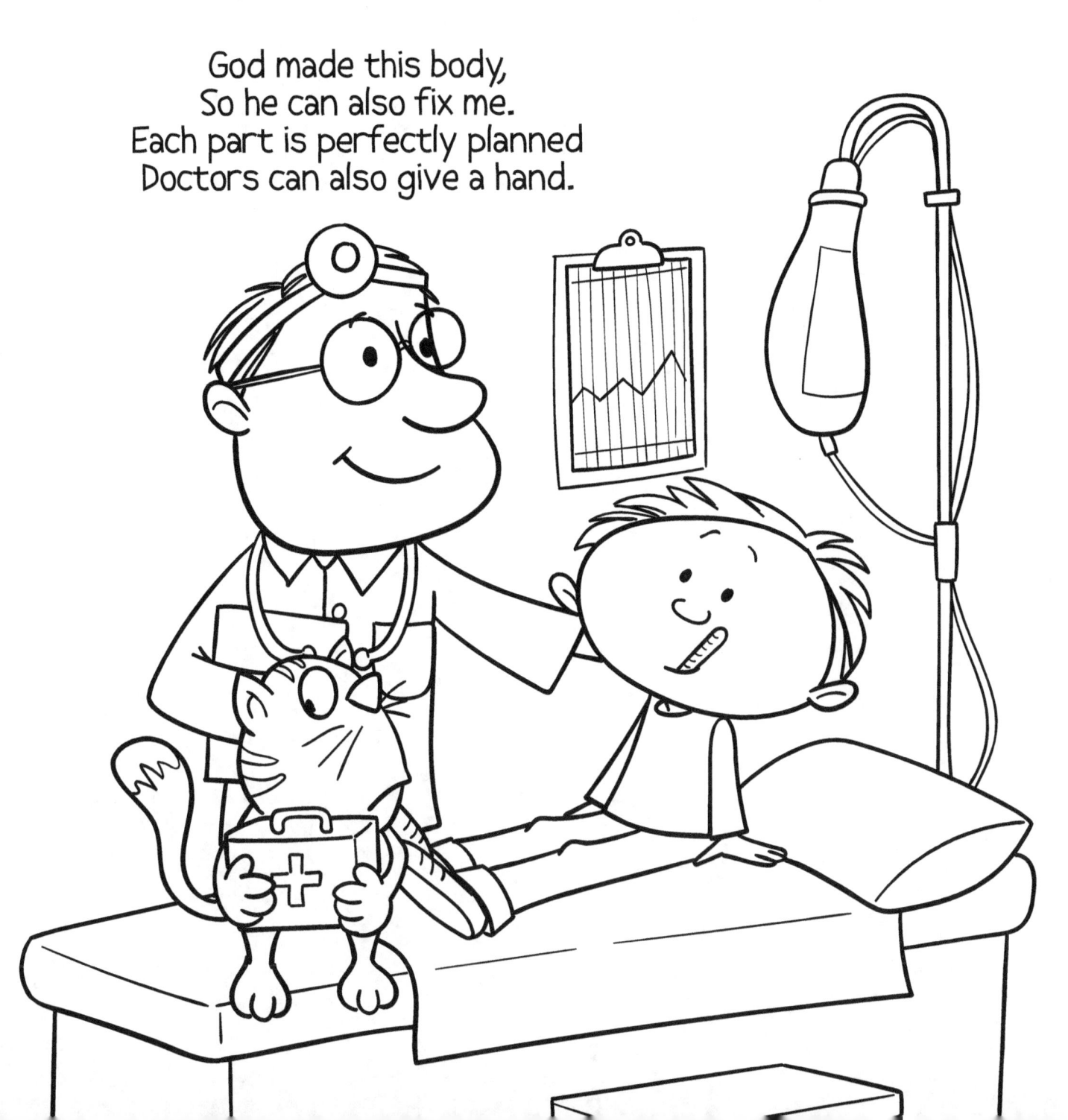

I pray for courage and grit
And faith that I will mend,
For strength to endure,
This sickness to the end.

Being sick is no fun
But it happens to everyone.
There's a time for sickness and tears
But then comes laughter and cheers.

Color all the items you might find at the hospital or that may be used at home while you're sick.

Help!

Find the words in the wordsearch that are listed below.

On my way!

```
R N I A P P E E S U H S I C K
E M E D I C I N E E L F C C W
T H Y O A E I P A D V F B O B
T V O E H M B L C H T A Y U S
E S P S A T I R O T C O D R M
B X K T P N L P L N D R N A R
T B I R G I E A D A U A H G E
E V O X E U T B E J D F R E G
G A X V E S P A B H Y F P E T
V B B L U B T S L Z A E H Q F
```

COLD
COURAGE
DOCTOR
FLU

GERMS
GET-BETTER
HEALING
HEALTH

HOPE
HOSPITAL
MEDICINE
PAIN

PEACE
REST
SICK
VITAMINS

Follow the lines to help the ambulance get to the sick boy.

Circle the 10 differences from these 2 pictures.

www.iCharacter.org

Published by iCharacter Limited ®. (Ireland)
By Agnes de Bezenac
Illustrated by Agnes de Bezenac
Copyright 2020. All rights reserved.
Proofread by Martine C. and team.

Copyright © 2020 by iCharacter Limited ®. All rights reserved. No part of this book may be reproduced in any form or by any electronic or mechanical means, including information storage and retrieval systems, without written permission from the publisher or author, except in the case of a reviewer, who may quote brief passages embodied in critical articles or in a review.

www.ingramcontent.com/pod-product-compliance
Lightning Source LLC
Chambersburg PA
CBHW081432070526
44586CB00020B/2563